Bon Appetit!

50 Salad Recipes

Barbara O'neill

Introduction

Traditionally, salads were vegetables, greens or mushrooms. They are served with dressing and spices. Now there are a lot of recipes. Everything depends on the traditions of a particular country and region. The main secret of a good salad is the dressing. It is prepared on the basis of some liquid components - vinegar, oil, lemon juice, soy sauce, yogurt or mayonnaise. It is the dressing that mixes all the ingredients into a harmonious whole dish. How to prepare simple, quick and tasty salads - read my recipes with photos!

Beef Heart Salad

Preparing for a celebration is always accompanied by pleasant troubles. How to decorate the house, where to place the guests and, most importantly - what to serve on the table? I'll tell you how I prepare this salad!

Ingredients

Beef heart (boiled) – 1 ½ cups
Beet (boiled) - 1 cup
Potatoes (boiled) - 1 cup
Carrots (boiled) - 2
Onion - 1
Ground black pepper - to taste
Salt - to taste
Mayonnaise - 200 ml
Pomegranate (grains) - 1 cup

Instructions

1. Finely chop the beef heart and peel the onion.
2. Grate the beets, carrots and potatoes on a coarse grater.
3. Place a glass in the center of the plate. It will allow to give the salad a ring-shape.
4. Lay out the potatoes, salt, pepper and add mayonnaise.
5. Next layers lay out the beef heart, onions and carrots. Add salt, pepper and a little mayonnaise.
6. Lay out the beets, salt and pepper again. Smear with mayonnaise on all sides.
7. Decorate the salad with pomegranate grains, thickly laying them all over the surface.
8. Carefully remove the glass and put the salad in the refrigerator for 1.5 hours.

Quinoa, Fried Eggplant & Feta Salad

Quinoa is now at the peak of gastronomic fashion. It is used to make soups, porridge, all sorts of salads and desserts. Try making a salad with fried eggplant and feta cheese. A great dish for anyone interested in good nutrition.

Ingredients

Quinoa (boiled) - 1 cup
Feta – ½ cup
Eggplants (medium) - 2
Herbs - to taste
Garlic - 2 cloves
Vegetable oil - 50 ml
Ground black pepper - to taste
Salt - to taste

Instructions

1. Dice the eggplants and soak them in salted water for 15 minutes.
2. Drain and dry the eggplants on a paper towel.
3. Heat oil in a frying pan, add the eggplant and fry until cooked.
4. Rinse the greens and chop finely.
5. Mix the cooked quinoa, fried eggplant, herbs, salt and ground pepper.
6. Add crumbled feta, minced garlic and mix.

Beans & Parmesan Salad

This quick salad will appeal to lovers of canned beans. Beans go well with Parmesan and juicy and flavorful cherry tomatoes.

Ingredients

Beans - 1 can
Parmesan – ¼ cup
Cherry tomatoes - 1 cup
Rocket - 1 cup
Olive oil - 2 tablespoons

Instructions

1. Cut the cherries into quarters and add the grated Parmesan.
2. Drain the beans and rinse, if desired.
3. Add the rocket, mix the salad and dress with olive oil.

Vegetables, String Beans & Tuna Salad

I love this recipe for its simplicity and originality. The combination of ingredients turns out to be very interesting. There are string beans, radishes, and other vegetables. And, of course, tuna.

Ingredients

Tuna - 1 can
Cucumbers - 1
Radish - 4
String beans – ½ cup
Quail eggs - 4
Cherry tomatoes - 6
Potatoes - 2
Olive oil - 2 tablespoons
Salad mix - 2 handfuls
Spices and seasonings - 1 teaspoon
Olives - 1

Instructions

1. Boil the quail eggs and cut in half.
2. Boil the string beans.
3. Cut the potatoes into small cubes and fry in olive oil.
4. Slice the cucumber and radishes into thin slices and the cherry tomatoes into quarters.
5. Mix all the ingredients together and season the salad.

Vegetables & Quail Eggs Salad

Quail eggs are perfect for salads: they cook quickly, look great,
and don't even need to be chopped. They go wonderfully with any fresh
vegetables and herbs, be sure to try this wonderful fresh salad.

Ingredients

Quail eggs - 6
Spinach - 1 bunch
Salad mix – 1 cup
Cherry tomatoes – ½ cup
Bell pepper - 1
Olive oil - 1 tablespoon
Salt - 1 pinch
Ground black pepper - 1 pinch
Oregano – ½ teaspoon

Instructions

1. Boil the quail eggs hard-boiled - about 4-5 minutes after boiling.
2. Let them cool in cold water, shell the eggs and cut them in half.
3. Rinse and chop all the greens, cut the cherries into quarters and the peppers into strips.
4. Mix the ingredients and dress the salad with olive oil and spices.

Mushroom & Melted Cheese Salad

Usually, salads with melted cheese are best for tartlets or snacks.
But this recipe with sliced marinated mushrooms is not like that at all!

Ingredients

Mushrooms (pickled) - 1 cup
Herbs - 1 bundle
Scallions - 1
Chicken eggs - 3
Melted cheese - 4
Mayonnaise - 4 tablespoons
Garlic - 2 cloves

Instructions

1. Boil the eggs and chop. Chop the marinated mushrooms in the same way.
2. Chop herbs, scallions and garlic. Grate the melted cheese on a coarse grater.
3. Mix the salad and dress it with mayonnaise.

Salad with Lemon Dressing

If you prefer light, fresh dressings, this recipe based on lemon juice will perfectly complement the taste of this salad. Add herbs, ground pepper and sea salt to taste to spice it up.

Ingredients

For the salad:

Chicken fillet - 1
Salad mix - 1 cup
Parmesan – ½ cup
Croutons - 1 cup

For dressing:

Lemon - 1
Olive oil – 2 tablespoons
Mustard - 1 tablespoon
Italian herbs - 1 teaspoon
Sea salt – ½ teaspoon
Ground black pepper – ½ teaspoon

Instructions

1. Bake, roast or boil the chicken to taste and cut into strips.
2. Place all the salad ingredients into the bowl.
3. Remove some lemon zest and squeeze out the juice.
4. Add the rest of the dressing ingredients and mix.
5. Add garlic to the dressing if desired. Pour over the salad.

Smoked Chicken & Strawberry Salad

If you like unusual culinary experiments, this salad with smoked chicken and strawberries is created for you. A great option to surprise guests and family during a home-cooked dinner.

Ingredients

Smoked chicken - 2 cups
Strawberries - 1 cup
Basil – ½ cup
Quail eggs - 8
Salad mix - 1 cup
Carrots - 2
Balsamic vinegar - 2 tablespoons
Lime - 1
Spices and seasonings - 1 teaspoon

Instructions

1. Boil the quail eggs for about 4 minutes, cool and cut in half.
2. Wash all the greens, grate the carrots and slice the chicken and strawberries.
3. Place the salad beautifully on plates, drizzle with balsamic and lime juice, and season to taste.
4. Garnish with basil leaves and lime slices.

Calamari, Avocado & Mushrooms Salad

Another simple and hearty salad. Prepare it with champignons or mushrooms and every time the flavor will be new. Try different variants and stop at the one you like.

Ingredients

Calamari (boiled) - 2
Champignons/Mushrooms - 1 cup
Avocado - 1
Chicken eggs (boiled) - 3
Onions - 1
Vegetable oil - 2 tablespoons
Mayonnaise - 2-3 tablespoons
Ground black pepper - to taste
Salt - to taste

Instructions

1. Slice the calamari, mushrooms, eggs, avocado and onion.
2. Heat the oil in a frying pan, add the mushrooms and fry until cooked through. Season with salt and pepper.
3. Mix avocado, calamari, eggs, onion and fried mushrooms.
4. Add salt, pepper and dress with mayonnaise.

Carrot & Calamari Salad

This salad turns out not too spicy, but you can add spices if desired. Onion is used in the recipe. Its role is to add flavor and aroma to the oil when frying.

Ingredients

Calamari - 2
Carrots - 1 cup
Onion – ½
Garlic - 2 cloves
Wine vinegar - 2 tablespoons
Vegetable oil - 3 tablespoons
Salt - to taste

Instructions

1. Put the calamari into boiling water, boil for 2 minutes and leave to cool on a plate.
2. Peel the carrots and grate.
3. Slice the cooled calamari and the onion.
4. Heat the oil in a frying pan, add the onions and fry until golden.
5. Mix the carrots with the salt, vinegar and pressed garlic.
6. Pour in the hot oil from the pan, straining it through a strainer.
7. Add the calamari, stir and put in the refrigerator for 3-4 hours.

Potato & Crab Meat Salad

If you think potatoes and crab meat don't go together at all, it's not true. To make it even more exotic, you can replace the cream with coconut or almond milk.

Ingredients

Potatoes - 3
Cream - 100 ml
Crab meat - 1 cup
Rosemary - 2 sprigs
Chicken eggs - 2
Parmesan – ¼ cup

Instructions

1. Boil the potatoes until tender and mix with the cream.
2. Separately boil the eggs and cut into cubes.
3. Add grated parmesan, crab meat and chopped rosemary.

Beans & Bell Pepper Salad

Tender beans are perfectly combined with crunchy bell peppers. And so that the salad is not too boring, I suggest adding a couple of secret ingredients.

Ingredients

Beans (canned) - 1 can
Lentils (canned) - 1 can
Chicken eggs - 4
Bell pepper - 4
Scallions - 1 bundle
Yogurt - 100 ml

Instructions

1. Boil the hard-boiled eggs and chop them.
2. Chop the peppers and chop the scallions in the same way.
3. Add the beans and lentils, mix the salad and dress with yogurt.

Beef Salad

This salad is good because it takes a few minutes to prepare.
You only need to roast the beef, which is very quick if you want to
keep it tender.

Ingredients

Beef - 1 cup
Salad mix - 2 handfuls
Lettuce – ½ bundle
Avocado - 2
Olive oil - 2 tablespoons
Ground black pepper – ½ teaspoon

Instructions

1. Roast the beef in one piece and slice thinly.
2. Mix the salad mix and shredded lettuce.
3. Add the avocado slices to the salad, pepper and drizzle with olive oil.

Smoked Sausage & Cheese Salad

It is a simple and quick snack, a salad with smoked sausage and cheese.
It is a good alternative to regular sandwiches if you don't like bread.

Ingredients

Smoked sausage - 1 cup
Cheese - 1 cup
Corn - 1 cup
Bell pepper - 1-2
Herbs - 3 sprigs
Olive oil - 2 tablespoons

Instructions

1. Finely and thinly slice the sausage and cheese, chop the herbs.
2. Slice the pepper and add the corn.
3. If desired, dress the salad with olive oil.

Mussel Salad

This salad has a very original combination of ingredients. It is almost classic Mexican cuisine, only with the addition of mussels.

Ingredients

Mussels - 1 ½ cups
Corn - 1 cup
Red beans (canned) - 1 can
Bell pepper - 1
Chili pepper – ½
Garlic - 2 cloves
Parsley - 4 sprigs
Lime – ½

Instructions

1. Fry the mussels until golden. Season to taste.
2. Finely chop the peppers, chili, parsley and garlic.
3. Add the corn and beans, mix the salad and drizzle with lime juice.

Pasta, Chicken & Mushroom Salad

Cold salad with pasta and chicken turns out to be very hearty and easily replaces the main course. For variety, I suggest adding mushrooms and something else to it. I will tell you about all the subtleties in the recipe!

Ingredients

Pasta – 1 ½ cups
Broccoli - 1 cup
Mushrooms - 1 cup
Chicken fillet - 1 cup
Spices and seasonings (for chicken) - 1 teaspoon
Olive oil - 2 tablespoons

Instructions

1. Dip chicken in spices and fry on both sides. Cut into strips.
2. Boil the pasta until cooked according to the instructions.
3. Separate the broccoli into florets and boil for a couple of minutes until tender.
4. Slice the mushrooms and fry until golden.
5. Stir the salad and season as needed.

Beans & Yogurt Salad

The highlight of this bean salad is the light and pleasant yogurt-based dressing. I'll tell you how to make it, and at the same time - what else to add to the dish. This salad is simple and flavorful!

Ingredients

Beans (boiled) - 1 can
Coriander – ½ bundle
Walnuts - 5 tablespoons
Purple onion - 1
Yogurt - 100 ml
Garlic - 2 cloves
Hmeli-suneli - 1 teaspoon

Instructions

1. Finely chop the onion, coriander and walnuts and mix with the cooked beans.
2. Add crushed garlic and spices to the yogurt. Stir and add to the salad.

Zucchini & Mushroom Salad

I especially recommend using chanterelles for this recipe. Zucchini is the highlight of the salad. This salad will surprise you and your loved ones!

Ingredients

Mushrooms (chanterelles) - 2 cups
Zucchini - 1
Cherry tomatoes - 1 cup
Salad mix - 1 cup
Gorgonzola cheese – ½ cup
Olive oil - 2 tablespoons
Ground black pepper - 1 pinch

Instructions

1. Fry the mushrooms until cooked through.
2. Cut the zucchini into circles and lightly fry on both sides.
3. Cut the cherries in half.
4. Add the salad mix and gorgonzola. Stir the salad.
5. Dress with olive oil and pepper.

Seafood & Radish Salad

A very unusual variant of seafood salad - with thin transparent slices of radish. If you wish, you can add mussels or other clams in shells, but it is not necessary.

Ingredients

Seafood – 2 cups
Salad mix - 1 cup
Radish - 1 cup
Chili - 1
Olive oil - 2 tablespoons
Spices and seasonings - 1 teaspoon

Instructions

1. Fry the seafood.
2. Thinly slice the radishes and chili.
3. Add the salad mix, season the salad and drizzle with oil.

Crab Sticks Salad

If you love seafood in any form, you'll love this salad. A little bit of vegetables and herbs to accentuate the flavor and that is all.

Ingredients

Mussels (marinated) - 1 cup
Shrimp (marinated) - 1 ½ cups
Seafood (marinated) - 1 cup
Crab sticks - 250 g
Olives - 1 handful
Garlic - 2 cloves
Onion - 1
Bell pepper - 1
Herbs - 4 sprigs
Lemon juice - 2 teaspoons

Instructions

1. Finely chop the bell pepper, garlic, onion and herbs.
2. Chop the crab sticks. Add shrimp and seafood.
3. Mix the salad and drizzle with lemon juice.

Seafood Cocktail & Greens Salad

Such a beautiful and spectacular salad is made of just seafood cocktail and some simple ingredients. Before serving, I advise you to decorate it with any favorite berries to taste, if you are not afraid of experiments.

Ingredients

Sea cocktail (canned) - 2 cups
Purple onion - 1
Herbs - 1 bundle
Chicken eggs - 2
Tomatoes - 2
Olive oil - 2 tablespoons

Instructions

1. Boil the eggs until cooked through and finely chop.
2. Chop the tomatoes and purple onions.
3. Cook all the herbs in a frying pan until tender and add them to the salad.
4. Stir and dress with olive oil.

Beef & Napa Cabbage Salad

For this salad you will need a lot of vegetables. The basis is napa cabbage, but feel free to add lettuce and other greens. And also some fresh vegetables and flavorful roasted beef.

Ingredients

Beef - 2 cups
Napa cabbage - 1
Cucumbers - 4
Tomatoes - 2-4
Herbs - 1 bundle
Soy sauce - 2 tablespoons
Olive oil - 2 tablespoons

Instructions

1. Slice the beef and fry until cooked through.
2. Chop the napa cabbage and herbs. Cut cucumbers into thin slices and tomatoes into slices.
3. Put the salad on plates and dress with olive oil and soy sauce.

Crab Sticks, Corn & Seaweed Salad

I love making salads. I can try different combinations of foods and make dishes to my liking. Recently, as a result of experimentation, I got this wonderful recipe. I advise you to try it!

Ingredients

Seaweed - 10 oz
Crab sticks - 1 cup
Corn (canned) - 1 can
Vegetable oil - 2 tablespoons
Salt - to taste

Instructions

1. Chop the crab sticks and seaweed.
2. Add the corn and mix everything, add salt, vegetable oil and stir.

Tuna, Avocado & Cucumber Salad

Salad with tuna, avocado and cucumber is a healthy and hearty salad.
It is a very simple salad, so it takes me only 10 minutes to feed my household
with a delicious salad.

Ingredients

Tuna - 1 can
Avocado - 1
Cucumbers - 2
Mayonnaise - 2 tablespoons
Spices and seasonings - 1 teaspoon

Instructions

1. Open the can, drain the oil or water if you are taking the tuna in its own
   juice. Slice the fish and put it in the salad bowl.
2. Cut the cucumber and avocado into small cubes and send to the fish.
3. Add mayonnaise, salt, pepper, add your favorite spices to taste. Mix well
   and treat your relatives. When serving, you can decorate with lemon
   slices.

Tuna & Avocado Salad

Quick, simple and very beautiful tuna and avocado salad will be a great appetizer for all occasions. It is impossible to resist such a delicate flavor.

Ingredients

Tuna (canned) - 1 can
Avocado - 1
Yogurt - 2 tablespoons
Dijon mustard - 1 teaspoon
Herbs – ½ bundle
Garlic - 1 clove
Spices and seasonings – ½ teaspoon

Instructions

1. Chop the garlic and herbs. I like it best with cilantro or parsley.
2. Dice the avocado.
3. Mash the tuna lightly with a fork.
4. Mix the ingredients and dress the salad with a mixture of yogurt and Dijon mustard.
5. Season it with spices to taste.

Crabsticks & Mussels Salad

For this quick and easy recipe, crab sticks are the best choice.
And mussels, the main thing is to properly and deliciously fry.
A wonderful diet snack!

Ingredients

Lettuce - 1 bunch
Mussels - 1 cup
Crab sticks - 1 cup
Sesame oil - 1 tablespoon
Soy sauce - 1 tablespoon
Ground pepper - to taste

Instructions

1. Fry the mussels in sesame oil for 2 minutes.
2. Season with pepper and mix them with soy sauce.
3. Slice the crab sticks and place all the ingredients on the lettuce leaves.

Fried Mushrooms & Beans Salad

Green beans are best for this recipe, but you can use any other legumes. But I advise you to boil them in advance or buy canned.

Ingredients

Beans (chickpeas) - 1 can
Mushrooms (chanterelles) - 1 cup
Coriander - 1 bundle
Garlic - 2 cloves
Spices and seasonings - 1 teaspoon
Olive oil - 2 tablespoons

Instructions

1. Rinse and clean the mushrooms well, chop them as needed.
2. Fry over medium heat until cooked through. For chanterelles, this is 15-20 minutes.
3. Add beans or chickpeas, chopped coriander and crushed garlic.
4. Season the salad and dress with olive oil.

Chicken, Cucumber, Tomato & Pecan Salad

I suggest using pecans for this salad. The flavor of this nut is sweet and very fatty. Thanks to this, it goes well with the rest of the ingredients.

Ingredients

Turkey breast (boiled) - 1 cup
Sun-dried tomatoes – ½ cup
Cucumbers (medium) - 2
Lettuce - 1 bunch
Nuts (pecans) - 1 handful
Vegetable oil - 2 tablespoons
Salt - to taste

Instructions

1. Slice the turkey breast, cucumber and sun-dried tomatoes.
2. Tear the salad leaves into bite-sized pieces.
3. Mix the salad leaves, turkey breast, cucumbers and sun-dried tomatoes.
4. Add nuts, salt, vegetable oil and mix.

Pineapple, Turkey & Corn Salad

Salad from pineapples with meat, different vegetables and greens, very tasty. Absolutely everyone can choose for themselves the most delicious option. Perhaps it will be a recipe with turkey and canned corn.

Ingredients

Turkey (boiled) – 1 ½ cups
Pineapple (canned) - 1 cup
Potatoes (boiled) - 2
Corn (canned) - 1 can
Ground pepper - to taste
Salt - to taste
Mayonnaise - 4 tablespoons

Instructions

1. Slice the cooked turkey, pineapple and peeled potatoes.
2. Remove the corn from the colander, rinse and wait for the water to drain completely.
3. Mix together the turkey, corn, pineapples and potatoes.
4. Add salt, ground pepper, mayonnaise and mix.
5. Place the salad on a plate, garnish with pineapples and sprinkle with chopped herbs if desired.

Seafood, Seaweed & Fresh Vegetables Salad

If you love seafood, be sure to try this recipe! Squid, octopus are good both boiled and marinated. I advise you to use pure seaweed without additives.

Ingredients

Seaweed - 1 cup
Squid (boiled) - 2
Octopus (boiled) – ½ cup
Tomatoes – ½ cup
Lettuce - half a bunch
Onion - half
Vegetable oil - 3 tablespoons
Lemon juice - 2 teaspoons
Ground black pepper - to taste
Salt - to taste

Instructions

1. Slice the calamari, octopus, tomatoes and peeled onion.
2. Tear the salad leaves into bite-size pieces.
3. Mix the seaweed, calamari, octopus, tomatoes, onion and lettuce.
4. Add salt and ground pepper.
5. Add lemon juice and oil and mix with salad tongs.

Lettuce, Spinach & Beef Salad

If you love greens and vegetables, this lettuce and spinach salad is made for you. The beef makes it a complete main dish for the whole family.

Ingredients

Beef - 2 cups
Lettuce - 1 bunch
Spinach - 1 cup
Cherry tomatoes - 1 cup
Olive oil - 4 tablespoons
Spices and seasonings - 1 teaspoon

Instructions

1. Roast the beef and slice into medium-thick slices.
2. Chop the lettuce, add the spinach and slice the cherry halves.
3. Season the salad to taste and dress with olive oil.

Fish & Mozzarella Salad

Salad with canned fish and mozzarella. I advise you to choose canned fish so that the dish is not too fatty. And for dressing, take a spoonful of olive oil.

Ingredients

Tomatoes - 2 cups
Mozzarella - 1 cup
Arugula - 2 handfuls
Corn – ½ cup
Canned fish - 2 cans
Italian herbs - 1 teaspoon
Ground black pepper – ½ teaspoon
Olive oil - 2 tablespoons

Instructions

1. Slice the tomatoes and mozzarella.
2. Mash the canned fish with a fork. Add the arugula and corn.
3. Season the salad and drizzle with olive oil.

Egg Salad

This is a very tasty and healthy salad, everything is impossibly simple!
I wish you a pleasant appetite!

Ingredients

Chicken eggs (boiled) - 2
Purple onion - 1
Spinach - 1 cup
Lettuce – ½ cup
Greek yogurt - 3 tablespoons
Ground black pepper - to taste
Salt - to taste

Instructions

1. Cut the lettuce and eggs. Peel the purple onion and cut.
2. Mix the salad leaves, spinach, fish and onion.
3. Add salt and ground pepper and mix.
4. Top with eggs and drizzle with Greek yogurt.

Fish, Fried Zucchini & Potatoes Salad

I love unusual salads, so I'm always trying new recipes and experimenting. In the course of my culinary search, I came across this dish. It is delicious, hearty and very original. You should definitely try it!

Ingredients

For the salad:

Red fish (boiled) - 1 cup
Zucchini (young) - 1
Potatoes (boiled) - 3
Spinach - 1 cup
Vegetable oil - 3 tablespoons
Lemon juice - 1 tablespoon
Ground black pepper - to taste
Salt - to taste

For dressing:

Olive oil - 3 tablespoons
Orange juice - 3 tablespoons
Mustard - 1 teaspoon
Honey (liquid) - 1 tablespoon

Instructions

1. Slice the boiled potatoes and lightly brown in a frying pan.
2. Cut the zucchini into circles and fry in vegetable oil until golden.
3. Cut the fish into small pieces and drizzle with lemon juice.
4. Mix the olive oil, mustard, orange juice and honey. The mixture should thicken slightly.
5. Mix in the spinach, fish, zucchini and potatoes.
6. Season with salt, pepper and pour over the prepared dressing.

Seaweed, Beetroot & Green Peas Salad

Make your diet more varied! Add healthy seaweed salads to your diet! For starters, you can try this simple recipe. If the vegetable is not sweet enough, add sugar.

Ingredients

Seaweed - 1 cup
Beet (boiled) - 1 cup
Green peas (canned) – ½ cup
Lemon juice - 2 teaspoons
Vegetable oil - 2 tablespoons
Ground black pepper - to taste
Salt - to taste

Instructions

1. Peel and dice the beet.
2. Mix the beets, seaweed and green peas.
3. Season to taste with ground pepper and salt.
4. Pour lemon juice, vegetable oil and mix.

Salmon & Orange Salad

Do you need a quick but original and unusual salad? Then this recipe with salmon and oranges is exactly what you need. I advise you to take lightly salted, smoked or marinated fish of your choice to get an amazing and unusual taste.

Ingredients

Salmon - 1 pack
Orange - 1
Olives – ½ cup
Spinach - 1 bunch
Salad mix - 1 cup
Feta – ½ cup
Olive oil - 1 tablespoon
Spices and seasonings - 1 teaspoon

Instructions

1. Cut the fish into strips, rinse the greens and drain the olives.
2. Peel the orange from the peel so that you only have the pulp.
3. Place the ingredients beautifully on plates and sprinkle with crumbled feta cheese.
4. Season the salad to taste and drizzle with olive oil.

Canned Pineapple & Chicken Salad

Chicken and pineapple is a classic duo that many people have already grown to love. Cut the products into cubes, add salt, pepper, mayonnaise and the appetizing salad is ready! This salad can be prepared for a festive table and an everyday meal.

Ingredients

Chicken - 1 ½ cups
Pineapple (canned) - 1 cup
Ground black pepper - to taste
Black pepper - 2 peas
Laurel leaf - 2
Salt - to taste
Mayonnaise - 3 tablespoons
Water - 1 liter

Instructions

1. Boil water, add black pepper, bay leaves and chicken. Boil for 20 minutes after boiling.
2. Cool the chicken and cut into small cubes.
3. Chop the canned pineapple in the same way as the chicken.
4. Mix the chicken and pineapple together. Add salt, ground pepper, mayonnaise and mix well.

Chicken Liver, Bacon & Croutons Salad

I have a lot of interesting recipes from chicken liver. This one, for example, I make often. Try to cook it just before serving, as the croutons quickly become soggy.

Ingredients

Chicken liver - 2 cups
Bacon - 1 cup
Lettuce - 1 cup
White bread – ½ cup
Black bread – ½ cup
Dijon mustard - 1 tablespoon
Vegetable oil - 3 tablespoons
Ground black pepper - to taste
Salt - to taste

Instructions

1. Slice the bacon into thin slices and tear the salad leaves into bite-size pieces.
2. Rinse the chicken livers and pat dry with paper towels.
3. Fry the liver until cooked through in a heated pan with oil.
4. Dice the black and white bread.
5. Dry the bread in a pan or use the oven.
6. Mix the salad leaves, bacon, chicken liver and croutons.
7. Season with salt and pepper, add the Dijon mustard and mix gently.

Fried Shrimps, Capers & Avocado Salad

I'd like to share this delicious salad with you. The recipe, of course,
I changed a little bit. So, here is a salad with fried shrimp, avocado and capers!

Ingredients

Shrimps (chilled) - 2 cups
Capers - 1 tablespoon
Avocado - 1
Cherry tomatoes - 1 cup
Butter - 1 tablespoon
Corn oil - 3 tablespoons
Lemon juice - 1 teaspoon
Ground black pepper - to taste
Oregano - 0.5 teaspoon
Salt - to taste
Herbs (micro) - a handful
Water (boiling water) - 1 liter

Instructions

1. Boil the shrimp, cool and peel off the shells.
2. Melt the butter, pour in the shrimp and fry for 2 minutes on each side.
   Sprinkle with oregano and ground pepper.
3. Peel and slice the avocados and drizzle with lemon juice.
4. Slice the cherry tomatoes in half.
5. In a wide salad bowl, combine the shrimp, avocado, tomatoes and capers.
6. Add salt, ground pepper, corn oil and mix gently.

Broccoli & Quinoa Salad

Useful quinoa can be added to soups, salads and pastries. Today
I am sharing with you a delicious salad with broccoli and quinoa.
It will appeal to everyone who is interested in good nutrition!

Ingredients

Quinoa (boiled) – ½ cup
Avocado - 1
Red beans (canned) - 1 can
Broccoli - 2 cups
Salad mix - 2 cups
Yellow tomato - 1
Blueberries - 2 tablespoons
Cashews (dried) – ¼ cup
Olive oil - 3 tablespoons
Lemon juice - 1 teaspoon
Ground black pepper - to taste
Salt - to taste

Instructions

1. Wash the broccoli under running water, dry it slightly and cut it into small florets.
2. Peel the avocado, slice and drizzle with lemon juice.
3. Drain the canned beans in a colander and rinse.
4. Cut the yellow tomato into small slices.
5. In a wide salad bowl, combine the broccoli, salad mix, avocado, quinoa, beans, tomatoes, blueberries and cashews.
6. Add salt, ground black pepper, and olive oil and mix gently.

Mussels & Croutons Salad

Tender mussels with crunchy breadcrumbs are rarely found in a salad. This quick and tasty salad decorate a festive table and will be appropriate even on a date.

Ingredients

Quail eggs - 4
Mussels (marinated) - 1 cup
Salad mix - 2 handfuls
Cherry tomatoes – ½ cup
Croutons – ½ cup
Olive oil - 2 tablespoons

Instructions

1. Boil the quail eggs for 4 minutes after boiling, let cool and peel.
2. Slice the eggs and cherry tomatoes, add the mussels and salad mix.
3. Drizzle with oil and sprinkle with croutons.

Napa Cabbage, Scallion & Lemon Salad

If you don't know what to make quickly from Napa cabbage – try a simple and affordable recipe of all possible. You only need green onions, lemon and your favorite spices.

Ingredients

Napa cabbage - 1
Scallion - 1 bundle
Lemon - 1
Salt - to taste
Ground black pepper - to taste

Instructions

1. Chop the Napa cabbage and the scallions.
2. Drizzle the salad with lemon juice and season.
3. Serve with lemon slices.

Tuna, Mango & Onion Salad

If you like exotic dishes, try making tuna, mango and purple onion salad. Sweet fruit is interestingly combined with fish. You'll need lightly salted tuna. You can buy it in the store or cook it yourself.

Ingredients

Tuna (lightly salted) - 1 can
Mango (ripe) - 1
Purple onion - 1
Herbs (to taste) - a couple of sprigs
Lemon juice - 1 teaspoon
Olive oil - 2 tablespoons
Salt - to taste

Instructions

1. Cut the tuna and peeled mango into small cubes.
2. Peel the purple onion and cut into half rings.
3. Rinse the greens and chop.
4. Mix the onion, mango, tuna fillets and herbs.
5. Do not forget to add spices to taste.
6. Dress with lemon juice and olive oil.

Crab Sticks & Pumpkin Salad

I'm sure it will be one of the most original salads with crab sticks on your table! And all because in this salad you need to add pumpkin. You need to bake the pumpkin slices with spices.

Ingredients

Crab sticks - 1 cup
Pumpkin – 1 ½ cups
Salad mix - 1 cup
Cucumbers - 4
Olive oil - 2 tablespoons
Italian herbs - 1 teaspoon
Ground paprika - 1 pinch

Instructions

1. Slice the pumpkin, drizzle with olive oil and sprinkle with spices.
2. Bake the pumpkin for about half an hour at 350° F.
3. Slice the cucumbers into circles and the crab sticks into large pieces.
4. Add the salad mix, pumpkin and serve the salad.

Chicken, Feta Cheese & Onion Salad

This salad includes fresh vegetables, olives and feta. But no one forbids you to experiment. Try this recipe and you will definitely like it!

Ingredients

Chicken fillet – 1 ½ cups
Feta – ½ cup
Olives (seedless) - a handful
Cucumbers - 2
Cherry tomatoes – ½ cup
Onion - 1
Vegetable oil - 1 tablespoon
Olive oil - 3 tablespoons
Oregano - to taste
Salt - to taste

Instructions

1. Heat vegetable oil in a frying pan and fry the chicken until golden on both sides.
2. Cool the fillet and cut into small pieces.
3. Slice the feta, cucumbers and cherry tomatoes.
4. Peel and chop the onion.
5. Mix vegetables, chicken, olives and feta.
6. Add salt, oregano, olive oil and mix.

Meat, Quinoa & Cherry Tomato Salad

Nowadays, it is fashionable to be healthy and watch your diet. Today, let's make a healthy quinoa salad.

Ingredients

Chicken fillet - 10 oz
Quinoa – 1 ½ cup
Seedlings - 1 handful
Cherry tomatoes - 1 cup
Salad mix - 1 cup
Pumpkin seeds (roasted) - 3 tablespoons
Vegetable oil - 2 tablespoons
Olive oil - 3 tablespoons
Ground black pepper - to taste
Salt - to taste

Instructions

1. Boil the quinoa for 5 minutes, drain in a colander and rinse.
2. Rinse the chicken fillets and cut into small cubes.
3. Heat the vegetable oil in a frying pan and lightly brown the chicken fillets.
4. Slice the cherry tomatoes in half.
5. Mix quinoa, chicken fillets, salad mix, cherry tomatoes, seedlings and pumpkin seeds.
6. Season with salt and pepper, dress the salad with olive oil and mix.

Potato, Tomato & Olive Salad

Salads with young potatoes are a separate pleasure. They are especially good for a picnic or for dinner. Sometimes I prepare this recipe with tomatoes and olives for the holidays.

Ingredients

Baby potatoes - 12 oz
Olives – ½ cup
Tomatoes - 2
Herbs - 1 bunch
Olive oil - 1 tablespoon
Spices and seasonings - 1 teaspoon

Instructions

1. Boil the unpeeled potatoes, cut into cubes and mix with olive oil and spices.
2. Dice the tomatoes, cut the olives into rings and chop the herbs.
3. Mix all the ingredients and serve the salad.

Beef & Arugula Salad

This simple recipe is a great way to diversify your everyday diet. I make this salad with arugula when I have a piece of roast beef.

Ingredients

Beef (baked) – 1 ½ cups
Arugula - 1 cup
Quail eggs - 6
Cherry tomatoes - 1 cup
Olive oil - 2 tablespoons
Ground black pepper - 1 pinch

Instructions

1. Boil the hard-boiled quail eggs, peel and cut in half.
2. Cut the cherry tomatoes and the beef into thin strips.
3. Add arugula and place the salad on the plates.
4. Add pepper and drizzle with olive oil.

Cucumber, Chicken & Pineapple Salad

A very interesting, light and fresh salad with cooked chicken, rice, cucumbers and pineapple. If desired, add garlic and spices to taste. This is a healthy and low-calorie recipe.

Ingredients

Chicken fillet - 1
Rice – ½ cup
Pineapple - 1 cup
Corn - 1 can
Cucumbers - 2
Cilantro – ½ bundle
Lemon (or lime) – ½

Instructions

1. Boil the chicken and rice until tender. Rinse the rice and chop the chicken.
2. Peel the cucumbers and chop the cucumbers together with the pineapple.
3. Add corn and chopped herbs to the salad and drizzle with lime or lemon juice. Mix all the ingredients.

Shrimp & Broccoli Salad

Large shrimp are best for this recipe. The finished dish turns out very tasty, but light and low-calorie.

Ingredients

Broccoli – ½
Shrimps - 10 oz
Lettuce - 1 bunch
Soft cheese – ½ cup
Cherry tomatoes - 1 cup
Mustard - 2 tablespoons
Honey - 1 tablespoon
Spices and seasonings (for shrimp) - 1 teaspoon

Instructions

1. Peel the shrimp and fry in the spices on both sides, 2 to 3 minutes.
2. Chop the broccoli into florets and cook in boiling water for about 5 minutes.
3. Dice the cheese and cut the cherries in half.
4. Place the ingredients on the lettuce leaves.
5. Mix the mustard and honey together and dress the salad.

Contents

Made in the USA
Las Vegas, NV
08 May 2024